you can't save her.

Angelica Ashley

To Pancake,

My forever writing companion,

I love you, my baby girl.

this is a book composed of poetry and stories written by a young girl whose only real safe space was writing. Please take care when reading as it is dark at times, specifically, themes of depression, anxiety, abuse, and even death at times.

Please be kind to yourself.

With that, shall we begin?

I will always be thankful
to the universe for granting my wish
and giving me a love unlike any other.
It was a beautiful dream,
                but we had to wake up.

/we couldn't stay asleep/

I was drowning
and you were shouting instructions on
how to build a boat,
yet when I finally got to land
by myself,
I still wanted to get back in that boat
with you.

I began drowning all over again.

/aftermath of the storm/

I couldn't hate you,
Even if I tried.
Just like you couldn't love me,
even if you tried.

/couldn't/

Promises filled me with hope.
But they were empty
thus making me empty.

/empty/

Sometimes I'll look down

and see the tiny scar you left,

and I'll remember

how tightly you hugged me

when you made the initial wound,

and the repetitive apologies

over and over,

and the laughs we had

about you hurting me without meaning to.

Each time I look at my hand,

I remember

the days you thought

the idea of hurting me was horrifying.

Each time I look at my hand

the pain shoots back.

Not from when the car door

slammed and locked on my finger.

But the pain of knowing that

you were no longer afraid of hurting me.

But much like the first time,

I was stuck,

unable to save myself from the pain

I knew I was in.

You didn't see what happened,

but you were still quick to remind me

that it is and will always be my fault.

/tiny scar/

My love was my power.
Your words were yours.

But my love was strong.
Your words trembled
as they left your lips
as if they knew what they were.

/lies/

and no one falls for the sad girl
and no one wants to spend their nights
listening to the girl cry
and no one would want to stay with that
and no one knows how to handle her
and no one wants to fight the fire
and no one is going to be her knight
because she isn't a princess
she is the dragon
speaking words like flames
that burn her each time
she opens her mouth
she cannot control it anymore

so she hides

on top of the tallest tower and soon

she will fall harder than she has
before

/the fiery tower/

It is a terrible thing to fall in love

Especially when that person decides
to fall for another
But remains "in love" with you

You are only cheating yourself, fool

/emotional affairs/

"maybe"

"who knows?"

"possibly"

I'm sure you are unaware

of how utterly terrifying those words are.

It is all uncertain, but I, for a fact, am certain

you are the one I want,

so, what do you want?

/possibly/

The one thing worse than losing the person
you care about most is knowing you're losing
them. You can feel them slowly distancing
themselves from you or you from them. You
can feel the fear building inside you. you
start preparing yourself for the worst, but
you know you will never truly prepared. You
start thinking about all the plans and the
future you'll never get. You feel yourself
giving up and you hate yourself for it, but
it's better than them giving up on you. you
leave first because you think it's better to
leave rather than be left. You tell them and
then try to be friends with them despite
knowing what is going to happen. Then one
day, it happens, and you feel numb because
you saw it coming. And it's your own fault
because you're the one who let it happen.

/the one thing worse/

He's screaming my name now.
I hear him.
He's waiting outside.
I'm supposed to be gone.
But I stuck around.
I want just another night.
Maybe I'll finally sleep.
You can take me away then.

/Him/

I don't want us running
after each other forever.
I'm afraid we'd get tired and give up.
Running is much too difficult.
I'd rather walk or jog.
It'd be better
if you were by my side
through
all the bumps, obstacles, or even fog.

But if you reach the finish line first,
and all your dreams come true,
I'll happily follow after you.

Just make sure you'll be there
waiting for me, too.

/marathon/

I feel rain pour down my cheeks
despite the fact I am indoors.
I wear my raincoat, and rubber boots,
and hold my umbrella so tightly
my knuckles turn white.
There is still water on my face.
I look up to see
if there are any leaks in the ceiling.
Nothing,
yet the floor has puddles.
I check
the sinks, and showers, and faucets.

Everything is fine.

I see the mirror above the porcelain

and I realize

it's from my own eyes.

/rain/

I hate how perfect you were.
I hate how kind you were.
I hate how you became important to me.
I hate that I slowly fell for you.
I hate that I did.
I hate how you didn't
and I hate that I don't hate you.

/hate/

I thought about it for a second,
no, a few seconds,
that turned into a few minutes
that turned to a few hours
that turned to a few days
that turned to a few months,
and here I am,
still thinking,
a year later,
and soon,
this year will turn into a few years
that will turn to decades
that will turn to centuries.

This thought may still be thought of even when I am not.

/thought/

When I moved, I thought
I was going to be sadder.
But it was actually fairly easy.
I guess maybe it's because
I was sadder to begin with,
When you've been at the bottom,
there's only one way to go.
Moving on has always been the dream.
And now I'm living it.

/big moves/

I didn't anticipate the fact
that I'd cry when you made me laugh.
It's just been so long
since we've had a moment
that was ours like that.
It hurt like hell to laugh with you.
All it takes is one scrape
to reopen a wound.

/don't die/

There is nothing I want more
than to just hold my love
and stare at it
in my hands
and see what we could've been.

There is nothing I want more
than to just be in love again
and to be loved again.

There is nothing I want more
than to be proven wrong
of my doubts and anxieties.

There is nothing I want more
than hold you one more time
and tell you all the things
I wish could be real.
There is nothing I want more than
nothing.

/nothing/

Tell me you love me.
Say it out loud like I've never heard.
Tell me you hate me.
You say it all the time proud.
Tell me you want me.
More than just like that.
Tell me, I mean something.
Anything, please.

/tell me/

Why am I the guilty one?

When you're the one who messed up.

She is a reminder of how you used me

and how I let you.

The only thing missing is an explanation

of why I'm on trial

when it was your crimes.

/mistress/

I know no contact is for the better
But I can't help but wish for
one more letter.
Maybe I'm still wishing for proof
that you do,
or ever did
love me.

/shared folder/

Dearest love,

When we meet you might fall for the
smile as others have before you.
Please, learn to love the eyes that cry
and the arms that long to hold you. If
you fall in love with the sunshine, I'm
afraid you'll be gone the moment the
rain arrives.

/sunshine/

I couldn't sleep
I kept thinking about
how much I loved
the idea of you.

/idea/

Even at the mention of your name,
I fall.
But not in the good way.

/downfall/

You were the first man I loved.
You left me promising you'd come back.
You left me crying,
and scared,
and screaming.
You left me with no explanation of why.
You left me and taught me the lesson
that love will never be enough.
That my love will never be enough.
You left me with a broken heart
and the belief that it was my fault.
You left me,
and now I live with the pain of
not knowing what is real
and what is not.

That was so many years ago
and my heart still hurts.
And I build barriers wanting to
save myself.
But it still wasn't enough.
It would never be enough.

/dad/

I'll regret you in the morning,

But tonight,

You're the only decision I want to make.

/in the morning/

I used to make fun of the girl

who'd fall asleep on skype

with her boyfriend

because I never understood

what that would do.

They're still not together in real life,

so, what was the point?

It wasn't until I found myself falling asleep to the small noises of tapping and buzzes coming from the other side of a phone that I understood.

When you love someone,

anything is everything.

/everything/

When I say I love you,
I am handing you
my heart and a dagger.
I give you the power to
do whatever you please.
I trust that you won't harm it,
but if I'm being honest,
you could pierce that heart
ten thousand times,
and it would still beat for you
and you alone.

/heart & a dagger/

The song that once
made my heart flutter,
now makes my heart stop.
I can't breathe.
I'm sobbing at the lyrics
that now sound more like wishes
to change what was inevitable.
The stars are fading
like words written in ink,
on tear-soaked paper,
that can never be rewritten.

/rewrite the stars/

Don't say

"I love you now."

Don't say

"all that matters is right now."

Don't say

"you have me now."

Don't say

"the future doesn't matter because you have me right now."

Because soon, "now" will become "then"

and we will be nothing

but two people with history.

Historians might as well erase our story

because it seems you have.

The past is the past.
The past is nothing.
The future is nothing.
All that matters is now.

You had me back then.
Now you don't have me.
Nor will you ever again.

/don't say/

Promises break and love fades.

People change and brick walls crumble.

Everything can become nothing,

If you have your priorities in a jumble.

/brick wall/

When I am not the sunshine

in a blue sky,

you run away from the flood.

It keeps raining, my love.

It just keeps raining

and the umbrella is nowhere to be found.

/the missing umbrella/

The clock is about to chime.
We are running out of time.
I might never see you again.
Maybe that's why I'm staring.
Trying to get a memory I can keep
for when I fall to sleep.

/out of time/

I compare thee,

to past sunrises and sunsets.

But still, those seem more beautiful

than your blinding light

that I endure out of love.

Am I losing my sight?

Your love burns and bruises.

But I endure it.

Your love is a small flame.

So easily put out.

Your love may be warm.

But you warn me to stay away.

I know it is dangerous.

Yet still I hold on.

The flame moves down, down, down.

I feel it reach the tips of my fingers.

/your love burns/

Forgive me, kind sir.
I hope you don't hate me.
I have written so many things
I do not mean.

I created her to be the vessel
of my most terrifying
thoughts and feelings
so I may be able to live
as who I truly want to be.

In other words, I write so I can be free
from the burdens of anguish
that trouble me terribly.

There is nothing beautiful
about the poems I've written.

They are written so
I don't completely lose
who I was before I lost you.

/forgive me/

I hear your voice speak your all.
I feel my knees begin to fall.
My bones shatter
as they touch the soft ground
you've laid down.
I reached for you.
You inched away.
I continued to fall anyway.

/the softest landing/

If you must know,

I am sitting in the dark alone.

Every night,

waiting to be found

before I completely disappear

into the darkness

that surrounds me.

/waiting to be found/

I held her.

I had her.

I loved her.

I lost her.

She was supposed to be mine.

She was taken away,

before she even arrived.

/she's gone/

I can't find you.
      I can't find you.

            Where are you?

Where are you?

/can't find you/

My heart was made of glass.

Housing all my weaknesses and strengths.

I let you in.

You decided

to shatter the walls.

I am covered in shards of thin white.

From afar it could look as if

I am swimming in diamonds.

But if you look closer,

the truth is

I am surrounded by the devastation

caused by loving an unforgivable storm.

/the greenhouse/

They're back.
They found me in the dark.
They're holding me so tightly.
I can't breathe.
I am silent.
I can't find the words to say.
They've taken them away.
They scream.
I feel their breath on my neck.
I'm dying all over again.
And I have no one to say goodbye to.

Love, what have you done?

You let them back in.
You didn't lock it on your way out.

They're holding me down.

I can't ever be free.

You hold both the lock and the key.

/the gate/

I should've made you promise

"don't fall in love with me."

I should've told you from the start

"you can't fall in love with me."

I should've realized way before you

"I am impossible to love."

I should've known what was to happen

"I hate you, I hate you, I hate you."

I should've seen this coming

"don't tell me you love me if you don't"

I should've been prepared for this

"I'm sorry, but I have to give this up."

/should've/

If I told you how it felt.
I swear, you'd swear
to never let anyone in the garden
again.

Because maybe,
it is better to be alone.

/lonely garden/

I am my own enemy.
I am the reason people leave.
I am the reason I am alone.
I am the reason and I alone.
I deserve everything.
I deserve everything.
I deserve everything.
I deserve everything.
I deserve everything
I get.

/my own enemy/

I was not loved.
She was not loved.
He was not loved.
Not by you, at least.

You were so loved.
You couldn't.
You couldn't love us,
You don't even love yourself.

/love yourself/

I'm still thinking about the way.
You said my name.
You smiled at my stare.
You held me in your arms.
You kept me warm.
You talked about the future.
You told me you loved me.

Sometimes I'll even hear it.
Sometimes I'll even feel it.
And then I'll remember
it's impossible to get it back.
You died so many months ago.
I miss everything you once were.

/you/

It's 1 am
and i read
what you said
Falling
asleep
in this bed
Can't get
you
out of my head
Wishing
to kiss
your lips red

In this
damned
hotel room so
I'm begging,
"just hold me."
I wished I wasn't the groom a while ago
But the wedding's tomorrow
At a nice church, with a nice girl,
in San Francisco

Don't pretend
you don't know
What you're doing to me
Don't act
all innocent

You don't have to be

You are all i ever wanted,
I think
I got nothing to give you
But tonight,
you'll be my something borrowed
So i won't be blue
And when I'm walking down the aisle
I'll just pretend,
it's you I'm walking to

I know
I'll never be the right man
you'll never be the right girl
you're not really here with me tonight
Tomorrow, when we dance, i'll miss
seeing your skirt twirl

And i'll marry her
She'll be
my beautiful wife
But i think we both know
you'll always be
the love of my life

/San Francisco/

I still have your charger.
You left it in my car.
I keep it by my bedside
though, using it is a war.

Most of the time,
it doesn't even charge my phone.
But it's nice having something,
I've already known.

If I got a new one,
It could break completely.
At least this one works some of the time
And that's enough for me.

I'll never admit it.

I'll never say it out loud.

Most days, I let the battery run out.

Breaks from trying, I think are allowed.

It's easier to live around the broken

than try to fix yourself.

I don't want to replace what you gave me

with a shiny new version on the shelf.

/broken charger/

You were always the sun.
I was never more than I was.
I never understood why
you always got the applause.
When we're one and the same.
Down to the flame.
So I told them all your flaws.

You burned too bright.
They loved everything
even how you'd respire.
Compared to you,
I was nothing, a little fire.

/little fire/

I don't know what I am.

I don't know what I want.

I am trying my best

to figure out how to deal with the storm

I have inside of me.

Without an umbrella

to protect me from the cold water,

I can't stop the thunder

from scaring me.

I can't keep my cheeks dry

from the streams of rain

that would fall.

But I can keep on walking

through it all.

/storm/

You let me go.
I kept walking,
thinking you were following
close behind.
You just stood still.
Waved goodbye
without any argument.
You let me go.

/let me go/

Just because

I closed the door.

It doesn't mean

I wouldn't let you back in

if you decided

to knock.

/please knock/

I've forgiven myself.

I've forgiven you.

I've forgiven

every single thing I've done.

I've forgiven

every single thing you've done.

But just because I've forgiven

does not mean I've forgotten.

/forgive/

I was okay

And then you.

You had to mess it all up again,

Didn't you?

/mess it up/

He convinced her.
It was fine, it didn't count.
She was still "innocent".
She knew he was wrong.
She knew it was all wrong.
But he said he'd marry her.
So, it didn't matter.

Just between you and her.
It can't be sin,
as long as it's love,
as long as he's happy,
as long as he loves her.
She's not wrong,
but it was all wrong.
Commitment meant it was okay.

If she waits,
he'll be "right"
and have his way.
She will want this.

Those 2 am pictures and calls.
Even in San Francisco,
you begged for her body,
but you never asked for her at all.

Was she ever important
Or did you like how she'd pant?
Like a bitch you could control.
She ignored her own voice
listening for your call.

Made backstage
her cage
nowhere to go.
How could the songbird sing
with your hand on her lips?

The moment you lead her
into that bed,
did you know what that meant?
That was all you ever wanted.
So, she gave it to you.
Hoping you'd learn to love the girl
whose body you loved
to grab in the dark.

That's all she was good for.
Then you'd walk out the door.
Leave her lying there
with nothing on
because she wasn't yours.

Commitment meant it was okay.
As long as its love.
As long as you're happy.
As long as you love me.
But you didn't love me.

Maybe for those few minutes you did,
but who would know for sure?
When you let me walk home alone
with nothing left of me.

I wasn't mine anymore.

/committed/

I am wandering in a museum
of everything that was once mine.
Every single item I pass is labeled
"do not touch."
I want to burn this place down.
These are mine, mine alone.
It seems I will never get anything back
and now I am nothing
but a stranger
visiting and viewing
art I created.

/the museum of me/

The garden is full and empty.
The flowers still bloom.
The grass is still green.
I let him go.
As I hold his crown in my hands
and the petals fall,
I look up and see everything
he helped create and destroy.
I wish I could write
how I felt in that garden alone
after telling him goodbye,
but how do you write that in words?

/the empty garden/

Each time I write, I wonder about
what would happen if this became
the last thing I wrote.
Would people read past writings
and think about
how messed up I must've been
To write this?
Would they feel the anguish
In each word written?
Would they understand
How it must have felt
To write such words?
Someone keeps knocking on the door

And I am writing my goodbyes.

Aren't I?

/last letters/

I don't know
what to do with these hands.
I could build you a house
with nothing
but hot glue, cardboard,
and rubber bands.

I'll never be smart enough
to be top of my class,
but I can teach you
how to safely break colored glass.
I can glue the pieces
and make a piece of art,
and when you eventually shatter it,
I can glue back together my heart.

I wish I could live
in a cardboard dollhouse
Do nothing but paint all day
and sew my own clothes
and make an easy bake soufflé.
My hands are tough
from slippery scissors
and cardboard cuts.
Glitter in my lungs
will be the death of me.

But if I could just paint prettier,
or sculp something profound,
or be better at everything,
or just anything I love.
I could be an artist

But I don't think I'm strong enough
to hold on to my ideas
when those close tell me,
it's cool but you'll never sell it.
Someone please tell me!
Who am I supposed to be?
Where am I supposed to go
if not away from here?
Sometimes I get the urge
to eat the yellow paint.
Maybe take the knitting needles
and stab them through my skin.
Sometimes I wish I could write
my own death so poetic,
they will have no choice
but look back and

remember me as an artist

/to die as an artist/

I believe there is
a perfect person for me
somewhere in the world
looking for me
while you keep trying to find me, love.
I'll do my best to find myself.

/find me, love/

This morning, I spent five minutes
looking myself in the eye.
Remembering
everything I need to get done,
that I want to do that I haven't done,
and all the things I have done
that I didn't want to do
and I can't find myself
sad or happy about either.
I merely exist.
Nothing else.
I am nothing.
A speck of dirt
in the universe.

/dirt/

One day,
She will smile.
Smile wide.
Smile big.
Smile true.

One day, she will smile again.
She will be smiling again
because of you.

/smile/

One day,

I'll find myself drinking tea,

singing songs,

and doing word searches

with someone in the morning.

Just smiling softly,

I'll see a sparkle in their eye

and I'll just know

that they love me

the exact same way

I love them

without any doubt

in our minds.

/morning tea/

One day,
I'll find someone
who'll take me to the moon
and when we're surrounded
by the beauty of the stars themselves,
I'll still be the one he's staring at.

/moon/

Today, I was happy.
Tomorrow, I don't know.
Today, I was happy.

/happy/

To the people:

- who tell me cheesy jokes
- appreciate my laugh
- who like my stories
- who play me nice songs
- who smile back
- who came back
- who hold my hand
- who pat my head
- who open their arms for me
- who believe I am enough
- who make me believe in love
- who make me love myself
- who make me want to stay alive
- who never gave up
- who give me high fives
- who inspire my art

- who bandage my heart
- who are yet to arrive
- who already said goodbye
- who are by my side

/to the people/

Beginnings and restarts.
You're really good at those.
Fixing broken hearts
with apologetic prose.

Words, words, words.
Enough to get me back.
One look in my eyes.
Make me lose track.

Promises were made
not one to throw things away.
I was going to hold you.
I was going to stay.

I was going to love you.
Even marry you one day.
I kept waiting for you
to meet me at the café.

Things changed,
now we're here,
talking at 2 am,
words so cavalier.
As I listen, I know
in my heart you remain.
Love doesn't leave,
it just doesn't stay the same.

Years have past.
Moments are memories.
Trying to find me
with online directories

Sometimes I miss you,
thinking maybe this time.
It will be different waiting
for the doorbell to chime.

I kept waiting for you
to change the storyline.
Waiting for you
to be the one begging to be mine.

Where did he go,
the man who wrote me rhymes?
Who was absolutely certain
I was worth the climb?

Promises I made
not wanting to be thrown away.
I was going to hold him.
I was going to stay.
I was so in love with him.
I wanted to marry him one day.

So, I waited, and waited, and waited
seven years later at that café.

I kept my promise.
But he never showed.

I finally walked away.
Let the coffee get cold.

/the café/

I think I'm finally in love

with someone:

- Who wants my love
- Who needs my love
- Who deserves my love
- Who will love me back

I think I'm finally

falling in love

With me

/in love/

Never your first choice,
but you knew I'd stay.
So, you kept me just in case
your sweethearts walked away.
I was your backup plan.
The pennies saved for a rainy day.

/coin bank/

Sometimes
I think about opening the door.
Once more,
just to see,
what could be.

I guess that's why
the coffin isn't nailed shut
because maybe the love I buried
could come back, but then what?

/the door/

I hope I stay there
in your mind.
Standing in your sweaters.
Hiding behind
the trees and the curtains.
Still sweet, pure, and kind.

I think you miss her
that girl who never wore brown.
The world glowed
with each spin of her gown.
The stars exploded
and the snow fell down.

And if I never see you again
it'll still be too soon.
The girl who spoke of magic and myths.
The voice that once made you swoon.
I think you miss her
like the sun misses the moon.

/the girl in the pink dress/

i'm a pretty penny. they pick up on the
street, they love and love and say i bring
them luck and that ive changed their life,
but the moment that they find a fountain,
they throw me away for a chance that
something better will happen. The chance! As
if the life i gave them, that we worked and
built together wasn't good, wasn't worthy,
was replaceable. And it feels as if every
drowning i endure, every body of water that
i find myself at the bottom of keeps washing
me away, i'm rusting and ruining, while they
run around searching for another me when
they discover that the wishes don't ever
come true. Until they clean the fountain and
i'm scooped out with the rest of the coins.
They dry us off and trade us for something
better and were sent out into the world
again. The quarters, nickels, and dimes, and
toonies and loonies, but i'm just a penny,
they don't even take me anymore, i guess
they were right

in the end, i'm not worth it,

am i?

/pretty penny/

You'll never know how it felt
listening to her cry
while struggling to sleep
under the watchful eye
of her three-year-old
and glow in the dark butterflies.

/mom/

My hair in the wind. I'm riding my bike down the street. I don't notice when you let me go.

My eyes tired. I'm falling asleep in your lap. I don't notice when you tuck me in.

My feet sore. We're dancing on my 18th birthday. I don't notice that it's just a dream.

Sometimes still, I'll sit on the windowsill and watch for cars and hope that it's you coming back from work. That's where you said you were going, so many years ago.

My memories of you are fading away like the dreams I have wishing you had stayed.

My tears stream down my face as I yell in the middle of the street, "Daddy, come back!"

I'm 5 years old. Mom called you back and you did return. I wanted to believe what I was told. That you would stay longer than however long it took for me to fall asleep.

You promised. After I begged you to stay or take me with you. But when I woke up, you were gone again.

The wind in my hair as the words, "Daddy, come back!" disappeared in the air. You were already hours away when I ran after you. My heart turned to glass that day.

With each heartbreak that followed, it always went back to you. I wonder who I'd be if I had a dad that stayed.

I know you and mom were never made to work, but you could've lived closer. Then my inner child wouldn't need a rework.

I'm so happy that you're happy now with
a family that makes sense, but do you
ever miss your baby girl who grew up on
the defense?

/no notice/

I grew up in a haunted house.

Kept the curtains closed,

passersby wouldn't know about the little girl lonely inside.

Kept quiet about the things in that house.

The demons hiding under the bed.

Laughter haunting me from across the hall.

The hands swinging and things thrown.

It felt at times like a never-ending game of hide-and-seek.

I'd hide in the closets

and pile the clothes on top of myself

till it felt heavy to breathe.

No one ever seeked me though.

Sometimes I'd sit and wait,

and wait,

and wait,

and wait,

and wait,

and most times I ended up

sleeping under it all.

I think I still carry the weight.

I feel myself breathing slower

and falling tired.

/haunted house/

I'll take care of myself
Like I have since I was four
I'll shut the curtains tight
Turn the lock on the door
When I move out
I'll know, I'll be okay.
Mom still brags about
My kindergarten days.
When I'd get myself ready
with no help
So, is it really a surprise
if I don't need you anymore?
I'm not new to being left,
I just thought maybe you'd stay.

Maybe I don't need the help,
but I'd like it anyway.
I like to live alone
but I wouldn't mind
building a home
with someone so kind.
No broken dishes
Or hidden away lies.
just good morning kisses
and blowing dandelions.

/kindergarten days/

When you look in the mirror
Who do you see?
When I look in the mirror,
all I see is
who I could've been.
Who I would've been
if you stayed.
If you just stayed,
if it was your hands holding me
up to the glow of the sun.
Who would I be if you stayed?
Maybe I'd be more shiny and fun.
I'll never know
because you went away,
left me all alone,
in less than a day.

Can you just be here?
I'm tired of the fighting.
Convincing myself
that you're really trying.
Everything would be easier
if you just stayed.
You say it's not about me,
is it just a charade?
I'll never know
because you went away,
left me all alone,
in less than a day.
I miss the old us
All I want is to go walking,
tell you about my day,
see you smile while I'm talking,

instead of that look
on your face when I'm crying,
followed by the sound
of my voice apologising.
So I'll say goodbye in empty hallways.
Leave tear stains on your shirts.
Watch the car drive off
then write about how much it hurts.
/by the window, watching you go/

Is this what happens?
Is this what happens
when you decide?
Nothing to do.
This fate is mine.
I'll lie in the grass.
Seep into the dirt
as the stars move
away from us.
The moon starts to cry.
I am gone.
I am right here.
I have left you.
I'll stay like a deer.
The light shining on my face.
I am grieving something

that hasn't died.
I am letting go of something
that hasn't left.
Make it make sense
if you're still here
like you say you are
then why can't I feel you near.
Weaken your grip
on the hand you're holding.
Let me fall back to Earth.
Let me miss the man on the moon.

/man on the moon/

I think about the first time
you touched me.
I think about the way you held me.
I think about how quickly you moved.
I think about how you moved so quickly
I couldn't even think properly.
I think about how it was the first time
I had ever gone over to a boy's house.
I think about how my intentions
were just to hold you.
Your hand, your face, your body.
Nothing more.

I just wanted to wrap my arms
around you.
Have you wrap yourself around me.
Nothing more.
I was so excited to sit in your room.
Look at the artifacts of who you were.
Even now, I have the details memorized.
The red paint, the closet doors
that opened when you'd close the other,
the posters, the knives you collected,
the tv I wanted to watch something on,
the bed you had me lie in.
I brought the script
we were supposed to rehearse.
I told my mom that we were going
to rehearse a script for drama.

I tried to practice
but your lips stopped me from speaking.
You turned it into something else.
I wonder who I could've been
if I had never walked down the street
on that sunny winter day.

If I never knocked on that screen door,
If I never walked past the fireplace,
the dining table,
the kitchen.
If I never introduced myself
to your cat.
If I never walked up those steep steps.
If I never looked at
the leftover Christmas decorations.
If I never walked past the collection
of fifty shade books on the shelves.
If I never went into your room.
If I never sat on your bed.
If I never let you see me.
If i never let you hold me.
If I never let you touch me.

You convinced me it'd be fine.
I believed you.
75%.
But it wasn't 75%.
It was 100% of me
that you took 25 days
after I turned 15.

You used my faith as a way to negotiate
how much of my body
I would be willing to give.
When I gave it to you,
you joked about it
"You might as well just go ahead
with the last 25%"

And now looking back,
I know I was scammed.
Everything changed after that.
I changed after that.

The child became a whore
and you let it happen,
and you cheered,
and you laughed,
and you looked,
and you guided my hands,
and you get to make jokes about me.

You ruined me

and you get to make jokes about it.

You ruined me

and you get to romanticize it.

You ruined me

and you get to forget about it.

You ruined me

and you get to get away with it.

/new year's day, 2018/

I feel like there are things inside of
my head. I hear them. The pitter patter
of their feet. They scream and scratch
at the walls. I shake my head to try
and get them out. All they do is scream
louder and louder and louder. So, I
cover my ears, but that does nothing to
help. They're in my head. I don't know
if I want them gone, but they're slowly
eating me away. It's just nature, and
nature is beautiful, but isn't beauty
pain? I remember when it started. I was
four years old, playing in the garden,
surrounded by dandelions. There it was
the bright red bug with the black dots
on its wings. It crawled on my finger;
I thought it was my friend. So, I let
it crawl up my arm, then it made its
way on my neck, it tickled, and I
laughed and then it found its way in
and made a home in my mind. It was
scary at first, but as time went on, I
stopped fearing it, and befriended it
instead. It multiplied, I don't know if
it had babies or invited friends over,
but the talking got louder and louder
and louder. And the pounding on the
walls got stronger. And that's when the

screaming started. It's been ongoing since, but sometimes it gets quiet. I get scared when that happens. I worry that they've left. But they haven't, I can't decide if I want them gone or not. They come back before I can make a decision about how I feel. I prefer the screaming over the silence.

Listening to them gives me comfort knowing I am never going to be alone again. As long as I have the ladybugs in my brain.

/ladybugs/

Sometimes I wish I could die before my time.

If I could be the flowers that wilt

when winter hits before

they have even bloomed.

The paintings left unfinished

by the greats.

Because if my story

could be left undone,

I could be left full of potential.

Frozen in time,

with nothing left to be said.

No failures, no expectations,

no disappointments.

Just me as I was

and who I could have been.

/the lady left in the fridge/

I'm leaving you alone now. I wish I could hold your hand through everything to come. I refuse to join you where you are. But you're dragging me toward a cliff I cannot climb. I'm untying the ropes and kicking away your hands. You will not drag me down. You will not take me with you. I am done. I am different. I am not going to follow your path. You could never be me. No matter how much you try to convince yourself that you could have done the same things as me. You could have never achieved what I achieved. You are nowhere near me. You do not get to stake a claim on the work that I did. I raised myself out of the mud you made. I fought like hell, avoiding the waves of the water, you tried to drown me in. You knocked me down, over and over and over and over, but I got back up. BY MYSELF. ME. I am who I am, not because of you, but despite you. I will be everything I dreamt of, out of spite. And I am okay with that.

/I'm leaving you alone now/

To love unconditionally,

truly unconditionally,

is to live with the pain

that you will never not love them.

No matter what harm they've caused.

No matter how many goodbyes.

How many fights?

How many wounds

opened and reopened

over and over until you ended up just ripped in half?

To love unconditionally

is to live

with the fact that

you will love them

longer than they'll love you.

Trying to balance

the love, the hatred, the resentment,

the heartbreak, the never-ending longing

for the person they were

when you loved them.

Before everything they did to you.

Before they hurt you.

Because before you even had the chance to change your mind and set some conditions,

they hurt you and now nothing, no rules, can apply.

You'll never truly know how far is too far until it gets to it.

I will love them.

No matter what.

I will always have love.

I just hope that one day

there will be someone

I will love unconditionally

who I will not need to ever forgive.

/the terrible curse of unconditional love/

Why couldn't there be a proper explanation?

Why do I have to live with the mysteries and ghost stories of what could have been?

Why did you have to tell me this beautiful story of perfection, and magic, and lies, lies, lies?

Of the house with the home studio

with the shelves of awards

and portraits of brightly painted happiness?

The crowds screaming our names.

My feet sore from standing

in front of them

soaking in the cheers and applause.

How dare you make me believe

I was destined for something more?

How could you write

such a wonderful dream

that I want to kill myself

if it meant I could stay

in that reality?

With the restaurant.
With the books.
With the songs.
With the tower
and the garden.
You tore it up,
and stomped on it,
and then burnt it,
and then walked away
as if it had been that way
when you found it.
As if you had nothing to do
with the damage
and then blamed me
for not writing something better.
Now I am nothing but boring.

I feel the need to share everything
with anyone willing to listen.
Because if other people find me
interesting or shiny
Maybe I can convince myself
I'm worthy of their attention.

/I'm boring now/

It's worse when it's no one's fault.

Losing someone when there's nothing or no one to blame.

So, I much prefer when I can be angry because it's easier to be angry than just sad at a loss that I suppose was always meant to happen.

/fault lines/

In another universe,
They got married.

/them/

A lonely birthday for you.
One at a table for two.
You're the only one singing
"happy birthday"
hoping your wish will come true.

/20/

My mom used to tell me to diet.
Exercise more. So, I could grow up to
be sexy. Like she was in the 90s. When
I tried on her red dress. That one she
won Miss Valentine in. A beauty
competition she still has the trophy
from.

It fit me perfectly. It was a zipper,
not a corset. It fit me. Why was I so
much bigger in my mind? I know in my
heart. I am learning to love my body.

But what if there was no reason to hate
it in the first place?

What if I looked at the tags?

What if I saw how they matched so
closely to my peers?

What if I didn't have this distorted
image? I spent my youth believing I
couldn't wear the same clothes as them.

What would I have worn?

Who would I have been?

Maybe I could have been more confident.

Maybe I could have learned how to be pretty.

Maybe I could have won a beauty competition in a red dress.

Maybe I could have been a healthier version of myself instead of spending all this time trying to slim down to fit clothes that already fit me.

/miss valentine/

When she was four,
She begged her mom to get dad back.
Mom called him.
He met them in a kfc parking lot.
They ate chicken.
She fell asleep in her dad's arms.
She woke up and he was gone.
It was too late.

When she was six,
She stopped believing in Santa
because he got her a ballerina barbie,
when she knew in her heart of hearts
that she had written down
that her only wish was
to get her dad back.

When she was eight,

she stopped believing in birthday wishes

because every year

guess who didn't show up

despite her never telling a soul what she wished.

When she was ten,

he did show up.

She walked downstairs.

He surprised her.

I think she cried.

It's funny,

she wishes he hadn't.

She wishes he could've just stayed
away.

The few days he was there

were more painful

than the years in between the visits.

She always knew

that in a day or two,

she'd wake up

he'd be gone again,

and mom would take her

to get some chicken.

When she was twelve,
mom got her a new dad,
who loved her so much
he'd kiss her on the lips
and he'd let her sit on his lap
until mom told her
not to do that anymore.

When she was fourteen,
she thought she found the perfect boy.
He felt safe and familiar,
it was like magic.
He was exactly what she dreamed about.
Except it wasn't.
Except it was.

He reminded her of someone.

When she was sixteen,
she was gone.
There was nothing left,
but a girl begging
for someone to want her,
holding onto the idea
that one day
he will surprise her
and come back to her.
She lived for the few days
that boy decided to visit her
instead of running after the others.

On the days, he didn't
with
her eyes puffy,
her cheeks and nose red,
she bought herself some chicken
and ate it right down
to the bone.

All because she loved a boy,
who reminded her of a man,
who left her alone.

/chicken bone/

Sometimes,

I wish you were dying,

just so I could forgive you.

/sometimes/

Sometimes,

I miss you,

but then I remember why I left

/sometimes II/

Sometimes,

I get scared he'll be like you,

But then he kisses my cheek

and does everything you never did.

/sometimes III/

I want to wake up in the morning and
make us hot chocolate. I want to help
you fold clothes and match the socks. I
want to have silly little fights about
which radio station to listen to on
road trips across the country. I want
to sit in the passenger seat because I
trust your driving more than my own. I
want to sit outside around a firepit in
our backyard and share or stories from
our younger days together.

I want to fall asleep in your arms

as you tell me the story again

of how you helped me save her.

/we saved her/

thank you for reading my book. <3

- Angelica Ashley Epino

Manufactured by Amazon.ca
Bolton, ON